Angels

Linda Proud

The Calling to Heaven of the Elect, *by
Luca Signorelli (c.1441–1523), San Brizio
Chapel, Orvieto Cathedral, Italy. In this
early 16th-century wall painting, angels
playing lutes, harps and viols receive
those about to enter Heaven.*

THE ANGELIC ORDERS

A belief in angels is shared by the three great monotheistic faiths of Judaism, Christianity and Islam. The source lies in the Zoroastrian religion of ancient Persia, which sees the universe as being divided between good and evil, an idea which became familiar to the Jews while they were in exile in Babylon. In the Jewish tradition, God, or *Yahweh*, is known as 'Lord of hosts', a host being an angelic army which fights evil and also performs certain other functions in the cosmos: guarding places and people, punishing wrongdoers, communicating the will of God and revealing God's word.

The Old Testament contains important sources of angel lore, notably the books of Genesis and Isaiah. The vision of celestial beings described in the book of Ezekiel, which includes references to the mysterious 'thrones', is also often interpreted as a vision of angels.

Christianity inherited much from Judaic tradition, and, in the New Testament,

Illumination from a 13th-century Jewish manuscript of the Pentateuch Haftaroth *by Eliyya bar Menathem, from Troyes in northern France. This shows six-winged Cherubim and Seraphim protecting the Ark of the Covenant.*

The nine choirs of angels are depicted in this Spanish manuscript of the Breviari d'Amour, *c.1400, by the Franciscan monk Matfre Ermengaud.*

angels attend many significant events, such as the birth of Christ and the Resurrection. By the time of St Paul there had arisen a cult in angels, which Paul condemned. However, the references to angels in both the Old and New Testaments are both vague and ambiguous.

A fifth-century text, purportedly by Dionysius the Areopagite, a disciple of St Paul, was the first attempt to categorize the various angels mentioned in the Bible, such as the Seraphim, Cherubim, and even the mysterious Thrones. This work, *Celestial Hierarchies*, which defines nine choirs of angels grouped into three orders, or hierarchies, is still the prime source of Christian angel lore.

Dionysius warned against taking visions such as Ezekiel's too literally. Angels, he said, are not golden beings or shining men flashing like lightning, but intermediaries between God and mankind more likely to appear in visions or dreams than as physical manifestations. They are seen when they need to be seen – and often by many people at once – but they have no bodily existence.

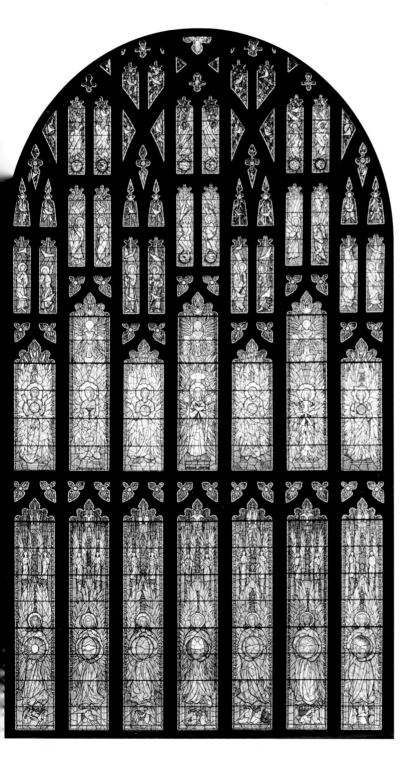

Stained-glass window, 1996, by Patrick Reyntiens, Southwell Minster, Nottinghamshire, England. This splendid piece of modern church art is based on the nine choirs of angels.

3

THE CELESTIAL HIERARCHIES OF DIONYSIUS: THE NINE CHOIRS OF ANGELS

First order
Seraphim
Cherubim
Thrones

Second order
Dominions
Powers
Virtues

Third order
Principalities
Archangels
Angels

ANGELS OF CREATION

Since everything we know about angels is based on visionary experiences, we have to rely on inspired writers and prophets for our information, and they do not always agree in the details. On the subject of when angels were created, some say before time and space, some with the stars, and others on the Sixth Day of Creation.

According to Thomas Traherne, a metaphysical poet of the seventeenth century, angels are 'spirits of light' who were brought into being when God created light. The heavens, which until then had been devoid of inhabitants, were, he wrote: 'in an instant filled with innumerable hosts of glorious angels, which were the morning stars and sons of God'.

Angels are commonly associated with light and, in the same way, Dionysius considered the Seraphim, Cherubim and Thrones of his first order of angels to be akin to fire. The Seraphim, who have three pairs of red wings, reflect the radiance of God and the fire of love and their function is to praise and glorify God.

The Cherubim, who have a single pair of blue wings, reflect divine knowledge, or wisdom. They are thought to be derived from the *Ka-ri-bu*, the monstrous guardians of Babylonian temples and palaces, and are first mentioned in Genesis, as guardians of the Tree of Life, east of Eden. It is ironic that, of all the angels, it is the Cherubim who have been sentimentalized as chubby baby angels.

The prophet Ezekiel described the Thrones, the seat of God, as fiery wheels with eyes, while the apocryphal writer Enoch described seeing 'a lofty throne' apparently made of crystal, with wheels like the shining sun. Dionysius interpreted Thrones as signifying Steadfastness.

Byzantine mosaic, c.1190, of the Last Judgement, on the west wall of the Cathedral of Santa Maria Assunta, Torcello, Venice, Italy. Wheels, Seraphim and Cherubim surrounding a Throne are shown above the central door.

4

5

The Angel Standing in the Sun,
by J.M.W. Turner (1775–1851),
was inspired by a passage in
Revelation where an angel
invokes birds of prey to feast
on the flesh of humanity.

Detail from Sir George Gilbert
Scott's memorial to Bishop
Wilberforce at Winchester
Cathedral, Hampshire,
England, showing an angel
holding the sun. Angels look
after the entire universe, not
just individual mortals.

The second order, the Dominions, Powers and Virtues, which St Paul mentions in his letter to the Colossians, is difficult to understand, and even Dionysius is not clear on the nature of these angels. This is perhaps why painters rarely portray them, an exception being the fourteenth-century Paduan artist Guariento, who showed the Dominions as enthroned, like kings, on marble; the Powers as holding devils in chains; and the Virtues as caring for pilgrims and ships, and performing miracles.

It helps to consider the choirs of this order in relation to those of the other orders. Thus, the Dominions are related to the Seraphim in the order above and to the Principalities in

The Angels in the Planet Mercury, *by Gustav Doré, c.1860–68. This illustration from 'Paradise' in Dante's Divine Comedy is the artist's attempt to show the infinite multitude of angels.*

the order below, and both reflect the love of the Seraphim. Dionysius refers to the Dominions as 'true lords'.

The Powers embody the laws of the cosmos and the workings of destiny and fate. In this way, they reflect the Knowledge of the Cherubim in the first order, which is then manifested in our world by the Archangels of the third order. According to angel lore, the forces of evil are fallen angels: Satan's followers are considered to be of the Powers, although Satan himself is said to be one of the Cherubim.

The angels known as Virtues have the task of infusing base matter with divine qualities and are thought to convey the blessings of God to mankind and to perform miracles. The word 'virtue', derived from the Latin *vir*, originally signified 'life force', or the quickening power of Creation.

A function of the second order is to separate the good from the bad, the guilty from the innocent. Dionysius suggested that this separation is manifested in our world by the Angels of the third order in the form of divine judgement. There are several such stories in the Bible; the Jewish festival of Passover, for example, commemorates the time when the Angel of Death, ordered to slay all the firstborn of the Egyptians, passed over the houses of the Israelites, which were marked with the blood of a sacrificed lamb.

The Angel of the North, *a steel sculpture by Anthony Gormley, spreads its wings over Gateshead in northern England, reflecting a sense of dominion over place.*

6

When the Morning Stars Sang Together *from* The Book of Job, *William Blake (1757–1827).*
God attended by his angels reveals himself to Job as the Creator of the universe.

ANGELS AND ARCHANGELS

The third order comprises the Principalities, Archangels and Angels, and it is this order which has contact with our world and mankind. The Principalities, which were mentioned in St Paul's letter to the Colossians, were described by Dionysius as 'benign princes' and are sometimes depicted as soldiers in battle.

Although only two Archangels (Michael and Gabriel) are named in the Old Testament, and two (Raphael and Uriel) in the Old Testament Apocrypha, there are actually seven Archangels according to Christian tradition, and many more in the Jewish tradition. Islam, however, cites only four.

Michael is the leader of the heavenly armies, and his role is to drive rebel angels from Heaven. His function is to engage with the enemies of the soul, and this on-going battle takes place as much on Earth as in Heaven. In the book of Revelation he is described as combating a great dragon 'called the Devil and Satan'. He is often depicted as a winged youth, clad in white or in armour, with lance or shield, slaying a dragon, and his association with dragons is celebrated at well-known Christian sites with Celtic origins, such as Mont St Michel in Brittany and St Michael's Mount in Cornwall. Michael is also a guide for souls of the dead on the journey to the hereafter, in which role he is depicted with a set of scales.

Raphael is associated both with healing and with death. One story, often represented in art, is that of Tobias and the angel, which appears

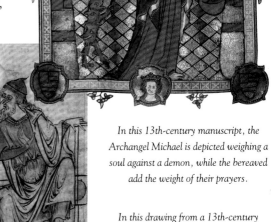

In this 13th-century manuscript, the Archangel Michael is depicted weighing a soul against a demon, while the bereaved add the weight of their prayers.

In this drawing from a 13th-century manuscript, the Archangel Raphael is shown healing the blind Tobit with a poultice made from the gall of the fish captured by Tobias.

in the book of Tobit in the Old Testament Apocrypha. This tells of a good man called Tobit, who, being blind, sent his son Tobias to collect money from a creditor in the company of a man called Azarias. As the pair walked beside the River Tigris, a fish leapt out to devour Tobias. Azarias bade him capture the fish, which would cure many of the problems

besetting Tobias's family, including Tobit's blindness. Eventually Azarias, revealed to be the Archangel Raphael, returned to Heaven. Because of this story, Raphael is often portrayed with a pilgrim's staff or carrying a fish.

The Angels, who comprise the ninth choir, are the heavenly messengers (see page 12) and have the closest contact with mankind.

The Paduan artist Guariento (c.1338–70) painted each of the nine choirs of angels. Here he shows the Principalities as an army of the Lord. (Museo Civico, Padua, Italy.)

GUARDIAN ANGELS

The idea that every living being has its attendant spirit is shared by many cultures: for the Romans it was the *genius*, and for the Persians the *jinn*, and, according to Plato, the souls of the dead were carried away by their attendant *genii*. Guardian angels are not mentioned directly in Judaeo-Christian tradition, but the idea has arisen from two passages in the Bible: one in Psalm 91 and the other in the gospel of St Matthew.

It has been suggested that an angel is the part of the soul that faces Heaven and acts only for the good. Ordinary people have ordinary angels, but great souls have angels from higher choirs. Muhammed's guardian angel, for instance, was Gabriel, while St Francis received the stigmata from one of the Seraphim.

The literature of encounters with angels is vast, and a surprising number of people, from a broad cross-section of society, will admit to

Guardian Angel, *by Giovanni Antonio Spadarino (c.1615–c.1650), shows the popular image of an angel looking after a child who is making its way over the treacherous path of life.*

Guardian Angel Holding the Hand of the Young Baptist, *by Giovanni Baronzio, Pinacoteca, Vatican, Italy. This 14th-century panel painting shows John the Baptist being guided by an angel during his infancy.*

experiencing angelic assistance or visions, including many who have no religious affiliations whatsoever. One of the most striking things about such stories – children rescued mysteriously from ponds or railway lines, men protected from muggers by a stranger, women helped through difficult childbirth by a suffused sense of well-being – is how abundant they are in this secular age.

If every person does have an angel guide – and some traditions speak of having two or more – then the invisible world must be very crowded. Also, according to the Prophet Muhammed, every created thing has an angel, even raindrops, which makes the number of angels beyond reckoning.

It is small wonder that medieval theologians expended so much intellectual effort on establishing how much space an angel occupies. In the end we must assume that, like an individual's mind or soul, an angel takes up no space at all.

*A Persian miniature, c.1540, from the Haft Paikar of Nizami,
shows the Prophet Muhammed being guided by Jibra'il (Gabriel)
and escorted by angels to Heaven where the prophetic lore will be
revealed. He rides on Burak, the Lightning.*

HEAVENLY MESSENGERS

It is no coincidence that both the Greek and Hebrew words for angel – *angelos* and *mal'akh* – mean 'messenger'. The angelic realm is the place which links God and our world – the meeting point of the heavenly and the mundane – and angels act as intermediaries, delivering messages between the two.

The messages which they deliver to mankind are from God, not from the angels themselves. Likewise, angels also carry the prayers of mankind to Heaven, and, according to medieval romance, this was the particular function of the Archangel Gabriel. Gabriel, above all other angels, is associated with the revelation of divine will: it was Gabriel who dictated the Koran to Muhammed, brought news of the impending birth of John the Baptist

This Romanesque carving on an apse capital at Chauvigny, France, shows the scene of the angel announcing the birth of Christ to the shepherds.

The terracotta sculpture of an angel from the workshop of Andrea Verrocchio (c.1435– c.1488), in the Louvre, Paris, France, is a fine portrait of an angel messenger.

to Zacharias, and appeared to Mary, the mother of Jesus.

All the major events in the life of Christ were attended by angels, but one of the most touching is the angel of the Lord announcing Christ's Nativity to the shepherds as they tended their sheep in the hills of Bethlehem. Described only in St Luke, this scene has been the inspiration for many carols and Christmas cards and may explain why many angels of medieval and Renaissance art seem to have a heraldic function, some even blowing trumpets.

Messages of a more lowly kind – the every-day prompts and reminders needed by mankind, and the warnings and the changes of direction – are brought by the Angels of the ninth choir of Dionysius, who are closest to us, and whose specific function is to communicate with us.

The Annunciation, by Fra Angelico (c.1400–55),
Monastery of San Marco, Florence, Italy. This subject has
been the inspiration of countless paintings, the best of which
capture a moment of profound communication.

ANGELIC INSPIRATION

From angels come inspiring dreams, prophecies and revelations, and the New Testament mentions several examples of such inspiration. Joachim, the father of the Virgin Mary, was told in a dream of the divine role of his daughter before she was born, just as Joseph, after discovering that Mary was pregnant, was told in an angelic dream not to abandon his marriage to her. Many of Joseph's subsequent actions, such as his sudden flight into Egypt with his family, just as Herod was planning the Massacre of the Innocents, were the result of his obedience to angelic warnings. Likewise, the Magi, or three wise kings, were inspired by a dream not to reveal the whereabouts of the Holy Family to Herod.

Books have also been inspired by angels. The Revelation of St John the Divine, which is full of apocalyptic imagery and symbolism, refers to itself as a book revealed to the author by an angel. The symbol of Matthew the Evangelist is a winged man, sometimes depicted as an angel communicating divine knowledge. Dante's *Divine Comedy* features angels at every major juncture of the progress of the soul from Hell to Paradise, while Blake's prophetic and visionary works are filled with angelic beings, and Milton's *Paradise Lost* is the drama of the heavenly conflict between good and bad angels.

Although the symbol of St Matthew is a winged man, this has been interpreted by artists such as Michelangelo Caravaggio (1573–1610) as being an angel. (San Luigi dei Francesi, Rome, Italy.)

Dream of the Magi, c.1130, by Gislebertus, Autun Cathedral, France. In this medieval sculpture, the three wise kings are shown asleep in the same bed and being inspired by the same angelic dream.

The idea of angelic inspiration being the source of poetry and music derives from the muses of the classical world. Whether coming from muse or angel, it is common for artists to ascribe their inspiration to agencies other than themselves. Classical poets often invoked the muse before beginning work, and angels may be similarly invoked – although this is not encouraged in the Christian tradition.

The Dream of Joachim, by Giotto (c.1266–1337), in the Scrovegni Chapel, Padua, Italy, shows the moment when the future is revealed in a dream to the father of the Virgin Mary.

In this drawing by Fantin-Latour (1836–1904), of Berlioz conducting the Requiem, the artist portrays the musician as being inspired by angels.

ANGELS OF ACTION

Although angels are popularly thought of as harp-players, and all sweetness and light, the stories of the Bible present a more active, often militant picture.

Angels sometimes appear in the form of guards, barring the way. For example, after expelling Adam and Eve from the Garden of Eden, God placed Cherubim and 'a flaming sword which turned every way' at the east of the Garden 'to keep the way of the Tree of Life'. Similarly, in the story of Balaam and his ass, Balaam took a journey against the will of God, only to find an angel barring his path. The ass turned off the road, and when Balaam beat it, it began to speak with the angel's voice, asking its master why he was behaving so cruelly. Balaam's eyes were thus opened to the presence of the angel, and he understood his error.

There are also examples of angels exerting violent retribution on the wayward. The fall of Babylon was brought about by a mighty angel taking up a stone 'like a great millstone' and casting it into the sea, saying: 'Thus with violence shall that great city Babylon be thrown down, and shall be found no more at all'. Before

Expulsion of Adam and Eve, by Hieronymus Bosch (c.1450–1516), Prado, Madrid, Spain. A sword-wielding angel drives out Adam and Eve from the Garden of Eden.

The story of Balaam and the ass was depicted in the earliest days of Christianity. Hypogeum of Via Latina, Rome, Italy, 4th century AD.

the depraved city of Sodom was destroyed by God in a rain of fire and brimstone, angels visited it in the guise of strangers and were given hospitality by Lot. These same angels struck blind the citizens who tried to force their way into Lot's house to abuse his guests, then, the following day, urged Lot and his family to flee the city before it was too late.

Equally violent is the story in Isaiah that tells how the Jews implored God for help against the Assyrians, and how the angels of the Lord, coming to their aid, destroyed over five thousand enemy soldiers.

Contrary to present-day sentiments, angels are not meant for the comfort of mankind but for its growth.

Jacob Wrestling with the Angel, by *Morazzone (1573–1626)*,
Archbishop's Palace, Milan, Italy. Although the angel refused to
answer when Jacob asked his name, he is thought to have been Uriel.

ANGELS AND THE AFTERLIFE

According to early Christian tradition, on the death of the body the soul moves on to a kind of limbo to await the final day of judgement. In the Middle Ages, however, a new teaching arose – that there was a particular judgement upon death, after which the soul was admitted to Paradise, Purgatory or Hell. As a result, one of the roles of angels became that of soul-carrier.

Towards the end of Shakespeare's *Hamlet*, Horatio says: 'Goodnight, sweet prince, and flights of angels sing thee to thy rest!' This idea of the role of angels being to guide the souls of the dead was particularly strong in the medieval and Renaissance periods, and many paintings from these times show angels bearing the soul, usually depicted as a baby or small person, away from the dead body.

The idea was revived in Victorian times, hence the familiar images of angels standing in cemeteries and by tombs. An echo of the angels that guarded the empty sepulchre of the risen Christ, they stand calm and reflective, reminding us that, while the body is mortal, the soul is immortal, and that after death it must take a journey with its angel guide.

A dramatic monologue of a soul leaving the body at death is *The Dream of Gerontius*, by John Henry Newman. Published in 1866 and hugely popular, it inspired Elgar to compose his masterpiece of the same name, which is commemorated in the splendid Elgar Window at Worcester Cathedral.

Angels have the role of recording a soul's deeds, of distinguishing the good from the bad, and of making judgement. In his painting

Detail from the Elgar Window in Worcester Cathedral, England, which captures the moment of the soul's departure attended by flights of angels.

The Reapers, *by Roger Wagner, is a modern work that restores angels to their full dignity.*

The Reapers, contemporary artist Roger Wagner, inspired by a line from the gospel of St Matthew, represents souls as ears of wheat being scythed by reaper angels. Far from the terrors of the medieval world, these winged peasants at work in an English field give death an air of profound stillness.

Detail from the Gate of Death memorial to the Melbourne brothers, by Baron Marochetti (1805–67), north aisle, St Paul's Cathedral, London, England.

HEAVENLY MUSIC

ome of the most enduring images of angels show them playing musical instruments or singing. This theme is especially strong in the art of the Renaissance, reflecting the belief then current that music and harmony restore the human soul. Since the primary function of angels is to praise God, it was only natural that church walls should be peopled with angelic musicians, playing not only harps but also kettledrums and bagpipes, lutes and viols, portable organs and other instruments of the time.

Just as art gave people a picture of Heaven, so music gave them the sound of it, and a chanted mass could fill a cathedral with heavenly music. Behind the sculpted figures on the west fronts of Salisbury and Wells Cathedrals, holes have been discovered that lead to a hidden gallery. Here choirboys once sang their responses, and, to those outside the cathedral, their amplified voices would have sounded like those of the angels and saints themselves.

People who have sung in choirs are often astonished by the experience of hearing 'angel voices' – for sometimes a choir sings a note with such resonance that its harmonic may be heard sounding an octave higher. Pythagorean theories of harmony could explain this as a numerical relationship heard in sound, but those with an ancestral memory from medieval times look up, half expecting to see a flutter of wings.

Angel playing
the bagpipes,
Thistle Chapel,
St Giles Cathedral,
Edinburgh, Scotland.

Angel playing kettledrums, from the Sforza
Hours, *an illuminated manuscript of c.1475.*

Angel Choirs, by Benozzo Gozzoli
(c.1420–97), from a fresco in the chapel of
the Palazzo Medici-Riccadi, Florence, Italy.